DSC SPEED READS

COMMUNICATIONS

Writing for Work

Moi Ali

GW00778348

DIRECTORY OF SOCIAL CHANGE

Published by
Directory of Social Change
24 Stephenson Way
London NW1 2DP
Tel. 08450 77 77 07; Fax 020 7391 4804
email publications@dsc.org.uk
www.dsc.org.uk
from whom further copies and a full books catalogue are available.

Directory of Social Change is a Registered Charity no. 800517

First published 2009

ISBN 978 1 906294 20 5

British Library Cataloguing in Publication Data

A catalogue record for this book is available from the British Library

Cover and text designed by Kate Bass
Typeset by Marlinzo Services, Frome
Printed and bound by Martins of Berwick

All Directory of Social Change departments in London:
08450 77 77 07

Directory of Social Change Northern Office:
Research 0151 708 0136

Contents

Introduction

Who will this book help?

Some people love writing. If you're not one of them, don't worry. You might never take pleasure from having to write at work, but you can at least take away some of the pain. If you lack confidence about how to write at work, and find writing a daunting prospect, this book is for you.

What will it give you?

Writing for work is very straightforward when you know how to approach it. This book will show you how to deal with the key workplace documents – from short and possibly ephemeral letters and memos to weighty reports. It includes quick tips on how to tackle the most common writing assignments, signposts for further information and exercises to help you put the theory into practice.

Chapter 1

Before you start

Writing for work need not be daunting. This chapter looks at why effective writing is essential for business success and what you need to consider before you begin.

At school you learned how to write essays. If you went on to higher education, you will probably be familiar with dissertations. However, few people are taught business writing skills and instead tend to rely on emulating colleagues (who were themselves probably never taught how to do it).

Business writing is characterised by a briefer, more concise style. Successful workplace writing rapidly gets to the point because busy individuals need to quickly understand your purpose in writing, and what you expect from them by way of action. Unlike a novel, which is bought for pleasure and eagerly devoured, a reader may regard reading a business letter or report as another chore.

Why effective writing is essential

Good writing:

- is more likely to be read (which is the whole point)
- is more likely to persuade, influence and inform
- helps avoid misunderstanding

- will boost your professional credibility and give you a reputation for clear thinking
- saves colleagues time when reading your work. (Managers in large organisations receive many reports and other documents. They are more likely to read and remember something that is well written.)

Conversely, poor writing makes you appear amateurish, lightweight and unprofessional. You will not be able to get your points across or achieve the outcome you hoped for. Resultant misunderstanding may lead to problems with relationships with your colleagues or customers.

What to consider before starting

Before you set pen to paper or mouse to mat, consider the following points.

- *Message*: What do you need to communicate?
- *Medium*: What is the best way to communicate your message? (By memo? Email? Letter?)
- *Audience*: Who are you writing for? (One named individual? A group of unknown people?)
- *Purpose*: What do you hope to achieve by writing? (Do you need to convey information or persuade someone to take a particular action? Respond to points raised in previous correspondence?)
- *Tone*: How do you wish to come across? (Friendly and approachable? Authoritative?)

Message

What are the main points you need to convey? Are there any secondary points? If you are writing about something controversial, you may also need to identify what you are unwilling or unable to cover.

Where next

For training courses related to writing go to the writing skills section of the DSC website at www.dsc.org.uk/Training/Personal development

Medium

Sometimes the medium is obvious. If responding to an email, it is likely that you will reply by email. But consider the alternatives. Part-way through lengthy email correspondence, it may become clear that each reply you send could generate misunderstanding or further questions. It is sometimes better to pick up the phone or meet to resolve matters face to face.

Audience

Remember your reader(s).

- Who are you writing for?
- How well (if at all) do you know them?
- How much do they know about the subject?
- How much time will they have to dedicate to it?
- Will that affect what you send to them?
- Where will your reader(s) be when they read your writing? (At a desk? Eating breakfast?)
- What will their mood be when they receive it?

Armed with this mental picture, write in a way that will meet their needs.

Purpose

Never write anything at work just for the sake of it. Always have a purpose in mind, whether it is to inform colleagues about a new policy, persuade your boss to agree to a proposal or convey information to an enquiring customer.

Tone

Make sure you do not unintentionally come across as cold, unfriendly and brusque in your business correspondence. Think about your tone. Write accordingly, carefully selecting a vocabulary that reflects your tone.

Top tip

Tone may vary over time, with a formal approach to a new business contact being replaced by a more relaxed style as you get to know them.

Sarah Westlake, Editor, MS Society

Chapter 2

Getting started

A blank sheet of paper can be daunting. This chapter will guide you through the five stages of writing, so that getting started will no longer be a problem.

Getting started can be the hardest part of writing. Where do you begin? How do you find the motivation? Just follow these simple stages.

The five stages of writing

1 Gather: Jot down ideas in any order.
2 Group: Arrange random ideas into clear themes.
3 Sequence: Organise themes into a logical order.
4 Draft: Come up with a draft.
5 Edit: Polish up your draft.

Gather

Scribble down thoughts and ideas. Do not censor anything – write it all down until you have run out of steam. This can help ensure that you do not overlook something important when you come to write, and it can unlock your creativity. If you omit this stage and immediately produce a draft, you will be concentrating on style and may miss important content.

Group

Organise thoughts into themes. Incorporate new ideas that emerge as you are doing this. Evaluate ideas and delete initial thoughts that you now consider irrelevant or unimportant. A structure should start to appear.

Top tip

It is always easier to cut out bad ideas than to think only of good ones, so let the ideas flow when you brainstorm and don't feel foolish about writing all of them down.

Janet Owens, Training Consultant

Sequence

Arrange your themes logically, whether chronological, alphabetic or some other helpful arrangement.

Draft

Produce a first draft. This will be edited and refined, so ignore style, grammar and syntax for now. Concentrate on getting words down on paper. Follow your emerging structure and fill in the detail. Relax and don't expect perfection just yet.

Edit

Set your draft aside, preferably overnight. Return to it afresh and start editing. How long you spend on revision will depend on:

- the length of your document
- how much is at stake (a letter seeking a £100,000 increase in your departmental budget might require more time and attention than a memo telling staff that canteen coffee has gone up by 5p)
- shelf-life and circulation (something that will be around for years, and read by hundreds, deserves more attention than a memo to a couple of colleagues).

> **Top tip**
>
> **Editing is the key to successful writing – whether business or fiction:**
>
> 'Writing is easy. All you have to do is cross out the wrong words.'
>
> **Mark Twain**

Dos and don'ts

- **Do** vary sentence length to add pace and interest.
- **Don't** overuse the same words or phrases, or repeat the same information.
- **Do** cut unnecessary words.
- **Don't** use clichés.
- **Do** stick to the pertinent and delete anything irrelevant.
- **Don't** omit anything important.
- **Do** check that what you say cannot be interpreted in different ways. Ambiguity creates confusion.

9

Editing checklist

☐ Have you achieved clarity? Ensure that your reader knows what you are saying without having to reread.

☐ Have you been consistent? If you have used 'ise' word endings (e.g. 'realise') do not switch suddenly to 'ize' word endings.

☐ Have you kept an eye out for jargon? Be sure that the intended audience will understand any you have used. If in doubt, explain it.

☐ Have you explained abbreviations at first use? Consider a glossary if necessary.

Creating readable chunks

Even short documents benefit from long passages being divided into readable chunks.

■ *Bullet points*: make long lists less off-putting and ensure listed items don't get lost in a sea of words.

■ *Subheadings*: break up text and help your reader navigate around your document with ease.

■ *Boxes*: in longer documents such as reports, boxed text can serve the dual purpose of breaking up your text and drawing attention to the boxed passage.

Remedies for writer's block

Writer's block affects all writers, professional and amateur. It can be an occasional complaint or an acute condition, but the remedies are the same.

■ Start writing, and don't worry if it's drivel. You can edit later. If you can't decide where to begin, get going with the undemanding parts. This will make it easier to face the difficult bits.

■ Do a different task for a while or take a complete break from work, such as a refreshing walk.

■ Tell someone what you need to write. It can help to clarify things in your own mind.

■ Sometimes writer's block is simply a case of lack of application. Get on with it and stop making excuses.

■ For a large or difficult writing task, prepare mentally by blocking off time in your diary.

Top tip

Faced with a large block of text on a page, people turn off. More and more, people are looking for their information in bite-sized chunks that they can digest.

Sarah Westlake, Editor, MS Society

Top tip

When facing a difficult piece of writing – a tricky letter or an important report – begin first thing in the morning when you're at your most fresh and alert.

Chapter 3

Plain English

This chapter describes the characteristics of Plain English, helps you to choose the right words when you write and rounds off with an exercise designed to help you put the principles into practice.

Some people think that Plain English is oversimplified, 'dumbed down', 'Janet-and-John' style writing. It isn't. Plain English is accessible, easy to read, clear, concise, unambiguous and unpretentious writing – the sort used in this book. Why, then, do so few people use it? There are various reasons.

- Pompous language makes the writer feel important.
- It's easier to hide behind obscure language.
- Some are concerned that Plain English is not an acceptable style in business writing.
- It can be hard to break rules that were drummed into you at school.

Officialese vs Plain English

Most business writers use what is disparagingly referred to as 'officialese' (see the following table).

Look at your own writing style and assess whether you use officialese or Plain English. If you use the former, it's time to change.

> **Top tip**
>
> To sound less formal and more friendly, consider using contractions (where you shorten two words, such as 'do' and 'not' to create 'don't'). Be careful not to overdo it.

'Officialese'	Plain English
Formal, sometimes pompous style	Informal and clear style - use inclusive language such as *you* and *we*
Uses the 'third person': the company, the organisation, the applicant (see next chapter)	Usually uses the first and second person: *I* and *you*
Contains jargon, unexplained abbreviations and acronyms	Uses everyday words and phrases. Avoids technical terms
Contains long, unbroken slabs of text and lengthy sentences	Contains short, readable chunks of text and shortish sentences. Uses bullet-pointed lists, subheads and summaries where appropriate
Uses long, obscure words and sometimes foreign and Latin words	Uses shorter words and avoids Latin and foreign words and phrases that are unlikely to be understood
Can be hard to follow because little account is taken of readers' needs	Follows a clear, logical order which shows an understanding of readers' needs
Uses passive voice (see chapter 4)	Uses active voice (see chapter 4)

Top tip

Avoid words of three or more syllables, as they are harder to recognise and read.

Dos and don'ts

Don't use long words – two short words are often preferable, e.g. 'make worse' rather than 'exacerbate').

Do use fairly short sentences (15 to 20 words).

Don't use jargon, abbreviations, acronyms or technical terms (unless they will be understood).

Do make sure that if jargon is unavoidable, you explain what it means.

As the case study demonstrates, the use of Plain English can improve an organisation's reputation by showing that its staff are human, not faceless bureaucrats.

Choosing the right words

Lazy writers accept the first word that springs to mind. Don't! Show-off writers choose long words believing that fancy vocabulary will make them look impressive – it won't. Choose words with care.

- Does your chosen word convey your intended meaning?
- Is it the right word to use in this context?
- Will your reader understand it? (Unfamiliar words interrupt the flow and cause readers to struggle. Replace unfamiliar and foreign words with everyday ones.)
- Have you chosen that word for the right reason? (To communicate, not to obscure.)
- Is there a better, more appropriate, more powerful or descriptive alternative?
- Is there a more succinct word? (Choose use, not utilise; live, not reside; try, not endeavour.)
- Does your choice of word or phrase avoid verbosity? (Instead of writing at this point in time, just say now. 'Regularly' is better than 'on a regular basis'.)

Exercise – officialese in action

This exercise shows 'officialese' in action and gives you a chance to translate it into Plain English.

1 Read the following letter.
2 Answer the questions that follow it.
3 Rewrite it. Make your version more concise, readable, clear and easy to follow, with a friendly and helpful tone.

Case study

One local authority found that bureaucratic letters to families demanding payment of deceased people's outstanding Council Tax bills were largely ignored. A more human letter, written in plain English, expressing sympathy for the bereavement, resulted in a big increase in Council Tax payment.

Where next

The Plain English Campaign, www.plain english.co.uk

13

Anytown Council
High Street
Anytown AT1 1AT
12th September 2009

Dear Ms Smith,

I acknowledge receipt of your letter dated 9th September 2009 and I am writing to advise that it is with much regret that the Council cannot accept the letter referred to above as a formal application for council housing. In accordance with Council policy (Rule 713/4), the only acceptable way in which prospective tenants may apply for council housing from this Council (other councils may well take a different view, but that is for them to decide) is to make a full written application via the Council's regulation housing application form (form SA/156438/a). I would like to point out to you that this can be obtained by calling in person at the Housing Department offices in the High Street during normal office hours which are 9am to 5pm, or by sending an SAE to this address should the applicant wish to apply for an application form by post. However, given the circumstances, in this instance I have taken the liberty of enclosing herewith, for your convenience, an official housing application form for completion by yourself, despite the fact that you did not include an SAE when you originally wrote to us on 19th April.

It must be recognised that with respect to the application form, it is imperative that all sections of it are fully, accurately and comprehensively completed if applicants wish their formal application to be given due consideration by Council housing staff. Failure to complete the application form as instructed will lead to Council personnel being unable to bestow the application with appropriate and timely consideration. Accordingly incomplete applications will be returned to prospective applicants forthwith by Council staff, thus unduly delaying or lengthening the application process and causing needless correspondence and resultant bureaucracy, which is in nobody's interests – neither the Council's nor the applicant's.

For future reference, I should be greatly obliged if you would direct any queries you might have pertaining to this matter to the undersigned or to the Council's Housing Officer, Mr Jones, who may be contacted by telephone on 01131 765 3232.

Yours sincerely,

L. Jobsworth

Mr. L. Jobsworth
Housing Assistant

Questions

- What impression do you have of the writer? What sort of a person does he appear to be?
- How do you think Ms Smith will feel when she receives this letter?
- What is wrong with Mr Jobsworth's letter?

Rewrite Mr Jobsworth's letter, avoiding his mistakes, then compare yours with the one below.

There is no 'right' way of improving this letter. Everyone will tackle it differently. The important thing is to:

- use Plain English
- be friendly, helpful and human
- be concise and avoid unnecessary information
- put yourself in the reader's shoes (in this case, by acknowledging that despite having gone to the trouble of writing you a long letter, Ms Smith now has to complete a form as well).

Where next

The Plain Language Commission, The Castle, 29 Stoneheads, Whaley Bridge, High Peak SK23 7BB. Tel. 01663 733177; www.clearest.co.uk

---

Anytown Council
High Street
Anytown AT1 1AT
12th September 2009

Dear Ms Smith,
APPLICATION FOR HOUSING
Thank you for your letter of 9th September 2009.
Unfortunately we can only accept applications on our official form. I appreciate that this may be frustrating, as I can see that you have gone to a lot of trouble in writing to us. Please complete all sections of the enclosed form so that our staff have the information they need to make a decision about your application.
If you have any questions call me or my colleague, John Jones, on 01151 765 3232.
Yours sincerely,

L. Jobsworth

Mr L. Jobsworth
Housing Assistant

Chapter 4

Style and grammar basics

This chapter advises on when to use initial capitals, explains apostrophe uses and abuses, sets out the benefits of writing using the first person and advises on how to write using the active voice.

Grammar geeks abound in the workplace. They are sticklers for spot-on spelling and perfect punctuation. While all these are important, do not get too hung-up if you don't know a pronoun from a preposition. Just make sure you get the basics right because rudimentary errors can make you look foolish.

Initial capitals

Much business writing is littered with wrongly applied initial capitals. Only use capitals when the words is:

- a proper noun (Edinburgh, Edith)
- a company or organisation name (Directory of Social Change)
- the first in a sentence.

If in doubt, leave it out.

Apostrophes

The phenomenon known as the greengrocer's apostrophe – *banana's 50p, pear's 60p* – is now so widespread that a properly placed apostrophe is almost as elusive as Lord Lucan.

Use an apostrophe:

- to denote possession: *the company's policy; the shop's opening hours; Steve's email*
- to indicate that something has been omitted: *'40s* (1940s – note that the apostrophe goes before '40' to denote that '19' has been dropped. It does *not* go before the 's' – 40's); *shouldn't* (should not).

Do not use an apostrophe:

- in familiar contractions: *phone* (short for *telephone*); *photo* (*photograph*)
- in the plural form of words ending in vowels in the mistaken belief that it will aid pronunciation (e.g. never write *camera's*)
- in straight plurals. The plural of *chair* is *chairs*, not *chair's*. However, if you wrote *The chair's broken*, that would be correct because it would be a contraction, short for *The chair is broken*
- in possessive pronouns – *its, ours, yours, hers, theirs*. The only exception is *one's*
- to denote the plural of an acronym or abbreviation. Write *The PCs in my office are old and need to be replaced*. (But *do* use an apostrophe to denote a possessive acronym or abbreviation – *My PC's performance is not good because it is old*.)

Apostrophe confusion

- *Children's* or *men's* – usually with a possessive plural, the apostrophe comes *after* the s (*the brothers' cat* – a cat belonging to some brothers). As *children* and *men* are plurals that do not end in s, simply add an apostrophe followed by an s to turn them into possessive plurals.

Where next

The Apostrophe Protection Society, www.apostrophe. fsnet.co.uk will leave you with a passion for this little punctuation mark. It also contains guidance on correct usage.

■ *It's/its* – *It's* is a contraction for either *it is* or *it has* (*it's* [*it is*] *a powerful computer; it's* [*it has*] *rained*). *Its* means belonging to it (*I have lost its lid*).

■ Names ending in s – (*James, Charles*). Whether you write *Charles's desk* or *Charles' desk* is a matter of personal choice. Just make sure you are consistent. The exception is when a name ends with *es*, creating an *iz* sound (*Moses*). In such cases use *Moses'* (it would sound odd as *Moses's* tablets).

The 'first person'

Traditionally, business writing used the third person (see the following table). This makes text less personal and more distant, which used to be the preferred style in business communication. Rather than write: 'You must tell us when you have . . . ' people would adopt a distant style and write: 'Applicants must tell the council when . . . '. Think of your writing as a written conversation between you and the reader. Use friendly, direct words such as 'I', 'we' and 'you', as you would when speaking to someone.

First person	The writer (or speaker)	I, we, me, us, my, mine, our, ours
Second person	The addressee (the reader or person spoken to)	You, your, yours
Third person	A third party (the person or thing spoken about)	He/she, him/her, they/them, it, the charity, their, theirs

Although the third person is best avoided, it is not banned. There will be occasions when you are stating your organisation's position or policy and it may be inappropriate to use the first person.

Active and passive voice

Active

The active voice is where someone does something.

'*Marianne sacked Jon.*' (three words)

'*The supplies division delivered the ringbinders.*' (six words)

Passive

The passive voice is where something is done to someone. The word order for passive sentences reverses.

'*Jon was sacked by Marianne.*' (five words)

'*The ringbinders were delivered by the supplies division.*' (eight words)

Word order

Active	Passive
1 Subject (Marianne, the doer)	1 Object (Jon)
2 Verb (to sack, a doing word)	2 Verb (to sack, a doing word)
3 Object (Jon)	3 Subject (Marianne, the doer)

> **Top tip**
>
> Be careful with the word 'we' in business correspondence. Only use it if expressing the agreed position of your organisation. 'I' is fine for your opinion; use 'we' when presenting your organisation's policy or position.

> **Top tip**
>
> Try not to worry about grammar and style in your first draft. Doing so will simply interrupt the flow. Correct errors when you edit your work.
>
> **Jacki Reason, Freelance Editor**

When passive is preferable

While you should generally aim to use the active voice, there are a few situations in which it is preferable to use the passive voice:

■ When you don't want to draw attention to something, such as a mistake. It might be better to say *A mistake was made* (passive) rather than *We made a mistake* (active).

■ When you do not know who or what the 'doer' is: *The Scotland football team was picked* (but you don't know who picked it).

■ When you need to be diplomatic, such as when you are dismissing, reprimanding or rejecting someone, or chasing unpaid bills: *This bill remains unpaid* is softer than *You have not paid your bill*. The passive can be less accusatory in this context.

Exercise – from passive to active

Turn each of the following sentences from passive into active ones:

1 A decision will be taken by the Council at the next subcommittee meeting.

2 Your home was visited last week by the Association's housing officer but she was unable to gain access.

3 An adopt-a-cat scheme is being run by the charity.

4 The Plain English chapter was found by readers to be extremely interesting.

Answers

1 The Council will take a decision at the next subcommittee meeting (or, even better: The Council will decide at the next...)

2 The Association's housing officer visited your home last week but she was unable to gain access.

3 The charity is running an adopt-a-cat scheme.

4 Readers found the Plain English chapter extremely interesting.

Where next

A Guide to Grammar and Style by Jack Lynch http://andromeda. rutgers.edu/ ~jlynch/Writing/ a.html

Chapter 5

Letters and memos

Most of us have received hundreds of business letters and memos, yet few of us are totally confident about writing them. This chapter flags up the key ingredients and shares top tips.

Business letters

Business letters are formulaic and therefore relatively easy to write. Every letter follows this pattern.

Key ingredients

- Date
- Recipient's name and (for business-to-business letters) job title and company
- Recipient's address
- Your reference number – if appropriate
- Salutation – *Dear Finance Director* (if you have no name, but have a job title), or *Dear Sir or Madam*; *Dear Dr/Mr/Mrs/Miss/Ms Bloggs* (if you have a name but do not know the person or have a formal relationship with them); *Dear Joe* (if the person is a close business contact or friend). It is a nice personal touch to write this by hand
- Heading with subject of letter
- Introduction – your reason for writing: *I am writing to you about...*

- Body text – your messages or any information you need to convey
- Closing – a way of summarising your main points, concluding and rounding-off your letter
- Signing off – use *Yours faithfully* if you do not know the name of the person you're writing to; use *Yours sincerely* if you know their name; use *Best wishes*, *Kind regards* or some other informal sign-off if you know the recipient well.
- Your signature, typed name and job title
- A list of any attachments or enclosures
- CC – this stands for 'carbon copy' and you should list anyone to whom you are copying your letter

Short letters are easier to read and digest, so keep yours to the point. The French scientist, mathematician and philosopher Blaise Pascal wrote: 'I have made this a rather long letter because I haven't had time to make it shorter.' He was right. Writing a long letter is relatively easy, but a short letter takes thought and effort. You need to pay attention to each word and assess what must be included and what can safely be omitted. Feel free to use subheadings to break up the text, and bullet points to give more emphasis to any points you make.

Never start every sentence with 'I'. Invert sentences to add variety. (For example the preceding sentence, inverted, would read 'To ensure variety, invert sentences where necessary' or 'Where necessary, invert sentences to ensure variety.) Inversion breaks the monotony of sentences beginning in the same way and will keep your reader alert and interested.

Memos

The memo, or memorandum, is one of the most common types of business communication. It is generally an internal document, usually brief, and often issued to a number of people at the same time.

Key ingredients

- *The heading*: 'Memorandum' or 'Memo' in large type.
- *Date*: The date of issue.
- *To*: The name of the person/people to whom it is issued – Fred Bloggs, or All staff.
- *From*: The name of the writer or sender (and job title if appropriate).
- *Subject*: A short, factual description of the subject of your memo.
- *Body text*: This is your message. Make it easily readable by using subheadings where necessary and bullet points for lists.

Uses

Use memos to inform staff of:

- *new information*: such as policy changes, new procedures, price increases or new staff
- *events*: such as staff meetings or seminars.

Ensure that your 'subject' line is informative and flags up urgency where necessary. If you write COMPANY BENEFIT SCHEME UPDATE, it might end up lying in someone's in tray indefinitely. URGENT: CHANGES IN COMPANY BENEFIT SCHEME REQUIRING IMMEDIATE ACTION is more likely to make them realise that they need to sit up and take notice.

Start your memo with a short paragraph explaining why you are sending it and why the recipients need to read it: *This is to update you on important changes to your company pension that require your urgent attention. Please read this memo and the attached booklet carefully, and make sure that you register by 12 October.*

For important memos that require the reader to take action, consider reminding them again at the end of the memo of what action is required and any deadlines. Use bold or italics to draw attention to key text that needs to stand out.

> **Top tip**
>
> Identify any attachments so that if they become separated from the memo, your reader will be aware and can ask for them.
>
> **Ben Wittenberg, Director of Policy & Research, DSC**

Chapter 6

Report writing

This chapter looks at the features of well-written reports, and ways to help make writing them a satisfying challenge rather than a daunting prospect.

Few people derive deep pleasure from writing reports. For most, report writing is a necessary evil. Whether or not we enjoy writing them, reports are vital to the functioning of most organisations. They provide directors and members with the information they need to take informed decisions, help with budget planning and keep stakeholders informed.

The best way to produce a really good report is to tackle the assignment from the reader's, rather than the writer's, perspective. When you are reading a report, what do you look for? What are the hallmarks of a well-written report?

Hallmarks of a well-written report

- Brevity and succinctness
- Logical order
- Well-argued proposals with supporting data
- Clearly identified risks, benefits and resources
- Unbiased opinions, with counterviews evaluated and presented

- Clear proposals, recommendations or next steps, with alternatives if appropriate

Now think about what is guaranteed to put you off reading a report. William Shakespeare was right when he wrote 'Easy writing is cursed hard reading.' The more effort you put into writing a concise yet comprehensive report, the easier it will be for your reader to understand. Conversely, the less effort put in by you, the more effort required by your reader.

Think about who you are writing for. Will it be a varied audience? If so, some readers may not be as familiar with the subject as you are. Your aim will be to write a paper that helps an uninformed reader to understand the issues as clearly as you do. When writing for an audience that is well versed in the subject and the issues, a more learned approach is required.

> **Top tip**
>
> The purpose of a report is to express, not to impress. Don't show off, just concentrate on communicating. That way you will impress by the way you have expressed.
>
> **Janet Owens, Training Consultant**

Key ingredients

Many organisations have a standard structure for reports. This is especially the case for papers being produced for a board or council. Common headings include:

- purpose – the reason the report was commissioned
- summary
- background – information on the background to the issue being written about, or summarising the history of that issue or concern
- main body – methods used, facts, discussion, results, alternatives
- conclusions
- recommendations
- financial or other implications (such as diversity impact assessment, communications implications)
- glossary and appendices
- bibliography or references.

Top tip

Charts and tables can aid communication. Visual messages such as graphs can convey complex information quickly and simply.

Top tip

Each report must be self-contained; do not assume that a previous report on this subject will have been read or remembered.

Maria Pemberton, Director of Operations, DSC

Not all reports contain all these elements. Decide which to include according to the convention in your organisation and the requirements of the report you are writing.

When asked to write a report for someone else, get a really good brief so you know what is expected. Ask for:

- a summary of why the report is needed
- key points or areas you need to cover
- issues to be avoided (if any) – for example, it may be that some areas will be covered in another report
- details of people you should consult (if any) or documents you should refer to
- an indication of length
- a deadline.

A good brief will ensure that you understand the need for the report and cover all the pertinent issues. It should save your time by ensuring that you know what is expected of you and so come up with the right report first time.

Report length

Would you rather read a long report or a short one? I can anticipate your answer. Some authors believe wrongly that a long report automatically shows them in a good light. Reports should be as short as possible. NASA offers advice on scientific reports on its website: 'Report quality is often inversely related to report length.' Don't pad out your report: just stick to the pertinent facts.

It can be difficult to decide what to put in and what to leave out. Include sufficient information and background material to enable your reader to understand the recommendations you are making or the conclusions you have reached.

Including excessive information or material that is only loosely related will obscure your recommendations, confuse the reader and waste everyone's time. Yet omitting contrary views may make your report appear one-sided. Present information in an honest way and strike a sensible balance between what needs to go in and what can be left out.

Consider including an executive summary in long reports. This is a brief outline containing enough information for the reader to understand the thrust of the full document without having to read it. Although by its nature the summary is short, pay it careful attention because it is likely that more people will read it than your full report.

Where next

How to Produce Inspiring Annual Reports, **K Burnett; K Weatherup, DSC in association with Burnett Works, 2000.**

Dos and don'ts

Do differentiate between fact and opinion.

Don't forget to explain any jargon and abbreviations.

Do use an appendix for information that is useful but not directly pertinent to your conclusions.

Chapter 7

Writing instructions

Well-written instructions are rare, yet writing accurate and useful instructions is not difficult. This chapter looks at the key ingredients of effective instructions.

Ever spent hours struggling to assemble a simple flat-pack bookcase? Instructions are maddening when they are ambiguous, unclear or omit vital details. When you write instructions for others, begin by putting yourself in your readers' shoes.

- What knowledge or background information will they have already?
- What can you take for granted and what will you need to explain?

Key ingredients

- A list of the contents where appropriate.
- An indication of how long it will take to complete, if appropriate.
- Checklists – such as necessary materials or equipment.
- A guide to troubleshooting – a list of potential problems and their solutions. Consider using a table showing these alongside one another.
- An FAQ (frequently asked questions) section – anticipate questions and provide answers.

Top tip

Consider including an instruction advising the reader to read through the full instructions before getting started.

- Footnotes or a glossary to define any words and expressions that you must explain in order to enable someone to follow your instructions (or you can include an explanation in the main text).
- A few examples to help explain to the reader exactly what you mean.
- Useful diagrams and illustrations.

Checklists

A checklist can help your reader prepare to follow your instructions. Consider one at the beginning, perhaps listing everything required to complete the form (or build the bookcase). For example:

'Before completing this form you will need:

- your child's birth certificate
- a letter from the head teacher at your child's current school
- the full address of the new school you wish your child to attend.'

A checklist at the end can help the reader check that everything has been completed and that they have not overlooked or forgotten anything important. For example:

'Remember to enclose:

- your rent book
- a cheque made payable to Anytown Housing Association
- a stamped envelope with your own name and address on it.'

Numbered steps

Numbered steps are logical and easy to follow. People are accustomed to reading about one step, performing it, then moving on to the next step. Such an approach

> **Top tip**
>
> Where instructions are long and complex, consider breaking them up into manageable sections so that they are less daunting for your reader.
>
> **Janet Owens, Training Consultant**

> **Top tip**
>
> Use a flow chart when there are several stages where the instructions path will divide, depending on whether the reader answers 'yes' or 'no'.

makes it easy for the reader to dip in and out. They can do the first two steps, take a break, and know exactly how far they have got when they return to the task. For example:

1 Draft your instructions.

2 When completed, set aside for a day or two.

3 Reread and make any necessary improvements.

4 Ask a colleague to read them with a critical eye, or consider asking someone to follow your instructions to see if they work.

5 Amend instructions in the light of any exposed ambiguity, omission or lack of clarity.

Where necessary, alert readers to any warnings *before* the step to which they apply. Make sure that your warnings stand out and cannot be missed, perhaps by using capital letters, large or bold text, or a warning or caution symbol.

Dos and don'ts

Do place illustrations alongside the text to which they relate.

Don't forget to explain what to do in case of a mistake or an unexpected result.

Do use plenty of headings and subheadings so that readers can find their way round your instructions.

Don't oversimplify and leave the reader lacking vital information, but do identify anything that is unnecessary and leave that out.

Do make sure readers can find their place again easily if they set the instructions aside to perform a step. That is where numbering and a clear layout can help.

Don't jump around. Follow a logical order, such as numbered steps.

> **Top tip**
>
> **Use diagrams, photographs, etc. in place of, or in addition to, words. A clear, labelled diagram can help a puzzled reader. Use the same labels in the text as in the diagram to avoid confusion.**

> **Top tip**
>
> **Keep instructions succinct. If you wish, include more detailed ones on your website, with guidance in your paper instructions on how to find them.**
>
> **Sarah Westlake, Editor, MS Society**

Chapter 8

Speech writing

This final chapter covers planning a speech, how to approach the all-important opening, what to consider in the middle and how to round the whole thing off.

A speech is written to be read aloud, so try to capture the relaxed informality and vitality of the spoken word. Stilted or awkward phrases, which fail to follow natural speech patterns, will jar when read aloud.

Preparation

Find out about: your audience, their knowledge and expectations; the subject and level of detail of your speech; other speakers and what they will be covering.

Establish the purpose of your speech. Is it to:

■ entertain, educate, inform or pass on information and knowledge

■ inspire the audience to take a particular action?

The purpose will set the tone and define the approach you adopt.

The opening

Aim to grab attention within the first 30 seconds because it is harder to win back an audience that has fallen asleep than it is to capture them at the start and keep them awake. Engage an audience with a:

■ thought-provoking question

■ relevant anecdote or story

■ controversial statement

■ shocking statistic or mind-blowing fact.

Top tip

Think about how your speech will be received by the audience as you read it. If you believe that a pause will be required to allow them time to digest what you have said or to applaud, write 'pause' in your speech to remind you to halt briefly.

Maria Pemberton, Director of Operations, DSC

Top tip

Never use a word in a speech that you feel uncomfortable saying aloud, even if you use it frequently when you write.

The middle

Now go on to develop your thesis and provide backup material to support your argument. Give some real-life examples to illustrate the point. Include a little light humour, if appropriate, though be sure not to offend.

The end

Aim for a memorable ending. Indicate that you are nearing the end, with phrases such as 'and finally . . .' or 'for my last point . . .' so that your audience knows what to expect. End with a pithy summary of your arguments or a witty anecdote that rounds things off. Otherwise complete the circle with a reference that takes you back to your opening remarks, or offer some further food for thought that will leave them pondering the subject long after you have left the podium.

Dos and don'ts

- **Do** use humour with care, as it is easy to cause offence and create embarrassment.
- **Don't** make too many points. Research shows that people remember very little from speeches and prefer simple messages.
- **Do** make your points clearly. When someone doesn't understand something they have read, they can reread it. With speeches, listeners can't re-listen
- **Don't**, when writing for someone else, use words or phrases that they would not use. Use language appropriate for the speaker and for the event.
- **Do** adopt a style that will suit the audience and the event. A humorous speech at a serious academic conference would be inappropriate, as would a serious speech at a colleague's celebratory retirement dinner.
- **Do** use a simple sentence structure that sounds natural when you read it out.

Top tip

Sentences that are easy to read in your head may not flow when you read them aloud. Read your speech aloud before editing, so you can spot what needs to be rephrased.

**Ben Wittenberg,
Director of Policy &
Research, DSC**